an extract from
maggie o'farrell's
after you'd gone
with an enthusiast's view
by rosemary goring

Scottish **Book** Trust

an extract from
maggie o'farrell's
after you'd gone
with an enthusiast's view
by rosemary goring

2003

Published by
Scottish Book Trust
Scottish Book Centre
137 Dundee Street
Edinburgh EH11 1BG

Tel: 0131 229 3663

**From April 2003 Scottish Book Trust will be moving its offices
to Sandeman House, 55 High Street, Edinburgh EH1 1SR.**

ISBN: 1 90107708 X
Copyright © Scottish Book Trust, 2003

Published with the support of the Scottish Arts Council National
Lottery Fund and The Hugh Fraser Foundation.

After You'd Gone is published by Review,
an imprint of Headline Book Publishing
ISBN: 0 7472 6816 9
Extract copyright © Maggie O'Farrell, 2000

Series design by Caleb Rutherford   eidetic
Printed in the UK by Cox & Wyman, Reading, Berkshire

contents

read **around books**

There is no shortage of fiction on the shelves of our bookshops – quite the opposite – but finding one that shouts out 'this is what you are looking for' is getting harder and harder as the number of books published goes up with each passing year. Too often we open a new book with expectation and enthusiasm only to discover disappointment and to struggle to get beyond page thirty. When we do find a book we really enjoy the urge is there to tell friends, colleagues and family to read it too in the hope that they will share our delight.

Read Around Books goes one step further and puts that enthusiasm down in black and white in the hope that many more readers will discover the joys of reading the very finest fiction that has emerged from Scotland over the last one hundred years. **This is a chance to sample before you borrow or buy**. Others have found these books before you, the writing held them spellbound and even when finished, these books would not let their readers go.

Each of the first twelve of these highly collectable little guide books promotes a work of fiction by a writer who lives in Scotland, was born in Scotland or who has been influenced by Scotland (our definition of Scottish is generous). Together they offer a marvellous introduction to the very best of Scottish writing from the twentieth and the first few years of the twenty-first centuries.

In each you will find a substantial extract, the enthusiast's view of the book, starting points for discussion for readers' groups, a short biographical piece about the author, and suggestions for similar reads which act as a further gateway to fine fiction.

Jan Rutherford
Series editor, 2003

the **enthusiast**

Rosemary Goring

Rosemary Goring is the Literary Editor for *The Herald.*

the enthusiast's **view**

After You'd Gone
By Maggie O'Farrell

After You'd Gone is a complex novel of many parts. A love story, a family saga, and a snapshot of modern life, it is also a tragedy, written with such deeply-felt emotion the reader comes to believe the characters are real, and the grief almost their own.

Juggling these elements with striking confidence for a first novel, Maggie O'Farrell holds them all together with a steely connecting thread whose tantalising clue is laid in the first few pages.

Starting out like a classic thriller, *After You'd Gone* sets the mood from the opening line: 'The day she would try to kill herself, she realised winter was coming again.' In that sentence we learn that the heroine, Alice, is in torment, and has been for a long time. For many months she has managed to resist the temptation to end her life, so what is it that pushes her to attempt it? All we are told is that on a spontaneous trip from London to Edinburgh, to see her sisters, Alice sees something, while in Waverley Station, which makes her finally lose the will to carry on.

What she has witnessed, we are told, was 'so odd and unexpected and sickening that it was as if she'd glanced in the mirror to discover that her face was not the one she thought she had. Alice looked, and it seemed to her that what she saw undercut everything she had left. And everything that had gone before.' She's barely been in the city for ten minutes, but she gets straight back onto a train to London, and once there, steps out – deliberately – in front of a car.

From that moment on, the novel is told in her absence, as she lies in a coma. It is a liberating device, holding the reader in perpetual tension, and allowing O'Farrell to jump between perspectives and voices as she unreels the complicated, fascinating story of Alice's life, and – equally important – that of her mother and grandmother before her.

Alice is a woman of around thirty when the novel opens, but O'Farrell takes us back to a time when her mother had not yet married her father, and was meeting her future mother-in-law for the first time. Sitting in Elspeth's comfortable house in the small, middle-class Scottish town of North Berwick, Ann cannot hide the fact that she is not in love with her husband-to-be. Ben, however, is besotted, and the marriage takes place, confining Ann to a life of domestic routine in the claustrophobic environment of a tightly-knit community, with Elspeth watching her every move, not so much from suspicion, but out of concern for her son's well-being.

Alice is the second child of three, dark-haired where Beth and Kirsty are blonde, strongwilled and wayward where they are biddable. From earliest childhood she rebels against her mother, disregarding her advice, almost wilfully aggravating her. At times she seems hellbent on destructive behaviour that harms herself more than anyone. Ann, in turn, treats her differently from her sisters, shrill and insensitive when trying to deal with her, unable to understand this child's awkward temperament. Her hot-headed handling of Alice sets up a spiralling web of resentment and frustration on each side which is to last until Alice is grown up and settled. At each point of conflict, Alice turns for comfort to her grandmother, whose calm, gentle advice is her greatest security. What Alice cannot know is that Elspeth harbours as many reservations about Ann as she does.

O'Farrell's descriptions of smalltown life are knowing and deft. Filling us in on Elspeth's own history, as the dutiful daughter of missionaries, whose own loving marriage was cut short by the war, she evokes the simmering curiosity of a town where very little ever seems to happen, where scandal is treated with shock, yet garnered with glee. From the very different perspectives of the respectable and motherly Elspeth and disappointingly cool daughter-in-law, O'Farrell draws a portrait of quintessential Scottish society in the second half of the last century.

In this environment Ann is doubly an outsider: English, with an accent she refuses to modify, and unfriendly. When she transgresses the unspoken moral code essential to the smooth functioning of society in this era, gossip and disapproval spread through the town faster than influenza. Only her family, it seems, remains oblivious to her conduct.

Though Ann is drawn with detail and some sympathy, O'Farrell concentrates her greatest skills on Alice, around whom the plot revolves. While she lies unconscious, her doctors offering little hope of her recovery, O'Farrell allows her the occasional first-person paragraph, to keep us connected with the present reality of the heroine. Mostly, however, she emerges through her past, which O'Farrell offers with verve and affection.

Alice is not an easy character to warm to. Spiky, sharp-witted, defensive, by her early twenties she seems to have wrapped herself in a protective barrier against men. We're given an unpleasant insight into her past romantic mistakes, episodes which we're led to believe have hardened her heart.

Two months into a new and exciting job in London, with a Literature Trust, Alice meets John, a journalist with a national newspaper. The attraction is immediate, but almost from the start the shadow of trouble lies over the relationship: John's father is an exceptionally traditional Jew and cannot accept his love for a gentile. His affectionate son will be forced to make the choice between his new love and his widowed father.

The description of John and Alice's growing love is an uplifting counterbalance to the pervasive melancholy and anxiety of the rest of the novel. Described with a verve and empathy that reveal the author as a true romantic, their passion ignites at first touch and retains its fire through the years. O'Farrell never quite manages to make Alice a loveable character, but John is likeable from his first appearance, and she gives him most of the best lines, seeming to warm to his winning spontaneity and humour, perhaps unwittingly rewarding him as richly as she can for falling in love with her very needy, but brittle, heroine.

For Alice, the discovery of John is the pivotal moment of her life. 'I loved him more than anything else I'd ever known. How was I to know he was a gift I couldn't keep?' Her grief for a love so deep is portrayed with almost tangible fervour. Cleverly gauging just how much the reader can cope with, O'Farrell allows us a glimpse into the depths of misery, but is wise enough never to lose the dramatic thread of her story, nor to forget to signpost the possibly shocking denouement that lies in wait.

Her manner of storytelling is sharp and direct, the novel told in snatches which are never more than a few pages long. Darting between North Berwick in the 1970s and contemporary London, between Alice at university and Elspeth at boarding school, between Ann as a child and Alice as a married woman, O'Farrell switches voices and tenses to fuse a dizzying kaleidoscope of emotion and fact. Creating a hectic, compulsive, page-turning momentum that matches the devastating and swift unravelling of family secrets, she resorts frequently to the present tense as a vehicle for immediacy, however historic the events described.

Though we are never allowed to forget that Alice lies in a hospital, the silent witness and victim of all this history, *After You'd Gone* is very much a novel of the past and the way its talons can grip those whose lives should be free and untainted. O'Farrell's fascination with the unpredictable, fascinating twists and turns of ordinary lives is one of her strengths as a novelist. Nobody is simply a cipher in this work, no-one placed there only to move the story from one point to the next. At the very least, her characters carry with them the hint of a fully rounded life; and in the case of her central cast, each is endowed with a complex life of their own, and with a believable, clearly delineated personality that transcends the workaday needs of plot-driven fiction.

Yet for all her fascination with the past, and with the lives and aspirations and failures hidden beneath the labels of grandmother or father or son, O'Farrell's novel draws its strength from the acuteness of her modern eye and her attention to contemporary nuance and detail. As we return for a last time to Alice's hospital bed, there is no doubt that this is a novel whose most powerful roots lie in the present, and – one hopes, for Alice's sake – far into the future.

The extract

After you'd gone

prologue

The day she would try to kill herself, she realised winter was coming again. She had been lying on her side, her knees drawn up; she'd sighed, and the heat of her breath had vaporised in the cold air of the bedroom. She pushed the air out of her lungs again, watching. Then she did it again, and again. Then she wrenched back the covers and got up. Alice hated winter.

It must have been around 5 a.m.; she didn't need to look at her clock, she could tell from the glow behind the curtains. She'd been awake most of the night. The weak dawn light cast the walls, bed and floor in greyish-blue granite, and her shadow as she crossed the floor was a grainy, unfocused smudge.

In the bathroom, she twisted the tap and drank straight from it, bending over and pushing her mouth into the pressurised, icy flow, gasping with the shock of the cold. Wiping her face on the back of her hand, she filled the toothmug and watered the plants on the bath edge. It had been so long since she'd cared for them that the parched soil didn't absorb the water, and it collected on the surface in accusing, mercuried drops.

Alice dressed quickly, putting on whatever clothes she found discarded on the floor. She stood at the window, looking down into the street for a moment, then went downstairs, slinging her bag over her shoulder, closing the front door behind her. Then she just walked, head bent, coat pulled around her.

She walked through the streets. She passed shops with drawn-down, padlocked shutters, street-cleaning lorries scrubbing the kerbs with great circular black brushes, a group of bus drivers smoking and chatting on a corner, their hands curled around polystyrene cups of steaming tea. They stared as she passed, but she saw none of this. She saw nothing but her feet moving beneath her, disappearing and reappearing from under her with a rhythmic regularity.

It was almost fully light when she realised she'd reached King's Cross. Taxis were swinging in and out of its forecourt, people milled through its doors. She wandered inside, with a vague idea of buying a cup of coffee, perhaps, or something to eat. But when she entered the white-lit building, she became mesmerised by the vast expanse of the departures board. Numbers and letters flicker-flacked over each other; city names and times were being arranged and rearranged in letters caught on hidden electronic rollers. She read the names to herself – Cambridge, Darlington, Newcastle. I could go to any of these places. If I wanted to. Alice felt up her sleeve for the bulk of her watch. It was too big for her, really, its face wider than her wrist, but she'd pierced the scuffed strap with extra holes. She glanced at it, then automatically lowered her arm again before realising that she hadn't in fact taken in what she'd seen. She raised the watch to her face again, concentrating this time. She even pressed the little button at the side that illuminated the tiny grey screen – where constantly shifting liquid crystal displayed the time, date, altitude, air pressure and temperature – in a bright peacock-blue light. She had never worn a digital watch before this. It had been one of John's. His watch told her it was 6.20 a.m. And that it was a Saturday.

Alice turned her face up again to the departures board. Glasgow, Peterborough, York, Aberdeen, Edinburgh. Alice blinked. Read it again: Edinburgh. She could go home. See her family. If she wanted to. She looked to the top of the column to see the train's time – 6.30 a.m. Did she want to? Then she was walking fast towards the ticket office and signing her name in cramped, cold-handed writing. 'The Scottish Pullman to Edinburgh' the sign said as she got on, and she almost smiled.

She slept on the train, her head resting against the thrumming window, and she was almost surprised to see her sisters waiting at the end of the platform in Edinburgh. But then she remembered calling Kirsty from the train. Kirsty had her baby in a sling and Beth, Alice's younger sister, had Annie, Kirsty's daughter, by the hand. They were straining up on tiptoe to find her and when they caught sight of her, they waved. Kirsty hitched Annie on to her hip and they ran towards her. Then she was hugging both of them at once and although she knew their boisterousness masked concern and she really wanted to show them she was all right, she was fine, the feel of both her sisters' hands pressing into her spine meant that she had to turn her head away and pick up Annie and pretend to be burying her face in the child's neck.

They hustled her to the station café, divested her of her bag and placed in front of her a coffee adorned with white froth and a sprinkling of chocolate. Beth had done an exam the day before and she related the questions she'd been asked and how the invigilator had smelt. Kirsty, trailing nappies, feeding bottles, jigsaws, Plasticine, held the baby, Jamie, in the crook of her arm while expertly harnessing Annie into a pair of reins. Alice rested her chin in her hands, listened to Beth and watched Annie cover a piece of newspaper with green crayon. The vibrations of Annie's strenuous efforts travelled across the table and up the twin violin-bow bones of Alice's forearms to reverberate in her cranium.

She got up and went out of the café to find the toilet, leaving Kirsty and Beth discussing what to do that day. She crossed the waiting room and pushed through the steel turnstile into the station Superloo. She couldn't have been absent from the café table where her sisters and niece and nephew were sitting for more than four minutes, but during that time she saw something so odd and unexpected and sickening that it was as if she'd glanced in the mirror to discover that her face was not the one she thought she had. Alice looked, and it seemed to her that what she saw undercut everything she had left. And everything that had gone before. She looked again, and then again. She was sure, but didn't want to be.

She bolted out of her loo, shoving her way through the turnstile. In the middle of the concourse, she stopped still for a moment. What would she say to her sisters? Can't think about this now, she told herself, just can't; and she slammed down on top of it something heavy and wide and flat, sealing up the edges, tight as a clam.

She was walking fast back through the café, reaching down beside her chair for her bag.

'Where are you going?' Kirsty asked.

'I have to go,' Alice said.

Kirsty stared at her. Beth stood up.

'Go?' Beth repeated. 'Go where?'

'Back to London.'

'What?' Beth sprang forward and seized hold of the coat Alice was pulling on. 'But you can't. You've only just got here.'

'Have to go.'

Beth and Kirsty exchanged quick looks.

'But ... Alice ... what's happened?' cried Beth. 'What's wrong, what's wrong? Please don't go. You can't go like this.'

'Have to,' Alice muttered again, and walked off to find the next London train.

Kirsty and Beth gathered up the children, their bags and the baby clutter,and hurried after her. There was a train just about to depart, Alice found, so she ran to the platform, her sisters following behind her, calling her name over and over.

On the platform, she hugged both of them. 'Bye,' she whispered. 'Sorry.'

Beth burst into tears. 'I don't understand,' she wailed. 'Tell us what the matter is. Why are you going?'

'Sorry,' she said again.

Getting on the train, Alice felt suddenly malcoordinated. The gap between the train step and the platform edge down to the tracks seemed to yawn wide into a huge, uncrossable crevasse. Her body didn't seem to be getting the right spatial information from her brain: she reached for the handle to pull herself across the crevasse, but missed, swayed and lurched backwards into a man standing behind her.

'Steady,' he said, and took her elbow to help her on.

Beth and Kirsty crowded into the window when she sat down. Kirsty was crying too now, and they waved frantically as the train moved off, running beside her for as long as they could before it picked up speed and their strides flagged. Alice could not wave back, she could not look at them and see their four blonde heads running beside the train, captured by the frame of the window as if on a reel of flickering Super-8.

Her heart was jumping in her chest so hard as she travelled that the edges of her vision pulsed in giddy sympathy. Rain screed back along the window. She avoided the eye of the reflection whizzing along beside her in another, reversed, tilted ghost carriage that skimmed over the fields as they hurtled towards London.

The air in the house felt icy when she got back. She fiddled with the boiler and thermostat, reading aloud to herself the incomprehensible instructions, peering at the diagrams bristling with arrows and dials. The radiators coughed and gulped, digesting the first heat of the year. In the bathroom, she stuck her fingers into the compost of the plants. It felt damp.

She was just about to go back downstairs, she thought, when she just sat down where she was – on the top step. She looked at John's watch again and was astonished to see it was only five in the afternoon. She checked it three times: 17.02. That definitely meant five o'clock. Her trip to Edinburgh seemed unreal now. Had she really gone all that way and then come back? Had she really seen what she thought she saw? She didn't know. She clenched her hands around her ankles and let her head fall on to her knees.

When she raised it again, the rain had stopped. There was a peculiar stillness about the house and it seemed to have got dark very suddenly. Her knuckle and finger joints ached, and as she flexed them they made sharp, cracking sounds that echoed round the stairwell. She hauled herself up by the banister and went slowly down the stairs, leaning her weight against the wall.

In the sitting room she stood at the window. The streetlights had gone on. Over the road a television flickered behind net curtains. The roof of her mouth felt swollen and bruised, as if she'd been sucking boiled sweets. Lucifer, appearing from somewhere, leapt noiselessly on to the window-sill and began rubbing his head against her folded arms. She smoothed the velvet of his throat with her fingertips, feeling the rumble of his purr.

She snapped on a light and the cat's pupils narrowed, like the closing of a fan. He jumped to the floor and circled her ankles, mewing loudly. She watched him as he prowled the room, casting sideways looks at her, swishing his long black tail. In the overhead light it was possible to see the ghost of a tabby in the monochrome sheen of his fur. Some recess of her mind told her: he's hungry. The cat needs feeding. Feed the cat, Alice.

She went through to the kitchen. The cat raced ahead of her through the door and began leaping at the fridge. There was nothing in the cupboard where she kept his food but a tired-looking cardboard box of cat biscuits and the brown rust-rings of tins long since eaten. She tipped out the box. Three biscuits fell on to the lino. After sniffing at them for a time, Lucifer crunched them delicately.

'Have I been neglecting you?' She stroked him. 'I'll go out and buy some catfood.'

Lucifer followed at her heels, aghast that she seemed to have changed her mind and wasn't going to feed him after all. At the front door, she got her keys and wallet from her bag. The cat slipped out of the door with her and sat on the doorstep.

'Back in a minute,' she murmured and clicked the gate shut behind her.

Maybe it was something to do with the rhythm of her steps hitting the tarmac or maybe it was being out among crowds of people again rather than in the cool, hermetic

interior of the house, but as she walked down Camden
Road to the supermarket it all started coming back to her.
She could see herself in that white melamine cubicle, walls
inscribed with skewered hearts and legends of love. She
could see herself washing her hands again at the stainless-
steel basin, sprayed with silver beads of water. She tried to
stop herself thinking about this. Tried to fill her mind with
other things, think about Lucifer, about what else she
could buy in the supermarket. She had leant on the
gleaming soap dispenser; lurid pink soap had coiled into
her wet palm, lathering into oiled bubbles under the water.
Behind her in the cubicles, two teenage girls had been
discussing a dress one of them was going to buy that day.
'Do you not think it makes me look a bit kind of flouncy?'
one had shouted. 'Flouncy? Well, now you come to
mention it.' 'Fuck off, fuck off!' What had happened then?
What had occurred a few moments later was so
disorientating, it was hard to order things in her head . . .
Did she need anything else? Milk, maybe? Or bread? . . .
Alice had turned then towards the hand-dryer and pressed
the chrome button, passing her hands over each other. It
had one of those little mirrors stuck to the front. She has
never really known why they do that. You're supposed to
be able to dry your hair if you turn the nozzle around, or
something, but she's never found the need to dry her hair
in a public toilet . . . What should she do when she got
back? Maybe she could read something. She could buy a
paper. How long is it since she read a paper
anyway? . . . The whole place had seemed reflective – the
shining porcelain tiles, the steel basins, the mirror above

them, and the mirror on the hand-dryer... Maybe she should call Rachel. She couldn't remember when she last spoke to her. Rachel was probably cross with her... The girls' voices had been bouncing off the walls. One of them had raised herself up onto the top of the cubicle and was looking down on her friend. Alice had, for some reason – why? why did she do that? – stepped closer to the hand-dryer, and the new angle made something behind her appear in the tiny square mirror... Perhaps Rachel wasn't talking to her. That would be strange. They'd never fallen out before. Perhaps she would get a basket at the shop, or a trolley, yes, a trolley would be good. She could fill it with everything she needed. Then she wouldn't have to go again for a while. But how would she carry it all home? ... Still with her hands under the hot jet of air, she had stared at the mirror and then, ever so slowly, so slowly that it seemed to have taken minutes, turned towards them.

Alice was by now standing at the pedestrian crossing. The green figure, legs parted in a purposeful stride, was illuminated on the traffic-light opposite. Over the road, she could see the supermarket; figures cruising through the neon-lit aisles. It seemed to her that her life was narrowing down to a vanishing point. People flowed around her, crossing the road, moving on. But she stayed still.

Someone nudged her in the back and she was pushed towards the edge of the pavement. The green figure was blinking on and off. Final stragglers were dashing across the road before the lights changed. The stationary red figure appeared and there was a moment of suspended calm before the waiting line of cars gunned their engines. As they powered past her, hurling fumes up into her face, their solidity seemed enviable to her – edgeless, slick constructions of steel, glass and chrome. The soles of Alice's shoes peeled away from the tarmac, and she stepped off the kerb.

part one

The only bit Alice can see of her father is the soles of his shoes. They are a faded brown, striated with the grit and terrain of the pavements he has walked. She is allowed to run along the pavement outside their house to meet him coming home from work in the evening. In the summertime she sometimes runs in her nightie, its pale folds catching around her knees. But now it's winter – November, maybe. The soles of the shoes are curved around the branch of a tree at the bottom of their garden. She tips back her head as far as it will go. The foliage rustles and thrashes. Her father's voice swears. She feels a shout welling like tears in her throat, then the coarse orange rope lowers itself, slightly coiled like a cobra from the branches.

'Got it?'

She seizes the rope's waxed head in her mittened hand. 'Yes.'

The branches shake as her father swings down. He lays a hand briefly on Alice's shoulder then bends to pick up the tyre. She is fascinated by the meandering rivulets that wander through its tread and the weft underneath its heavy black rubber. 'That's what holds it together,' the man at the shop had told her. The sudden scraped bald patch in the middle of the meanders makes her shudder but she doesn't quite know why. Her father winds the orange rope around the tyre and makes a thick, twisted knot.

'Can I have a go now?' Her hands grip the tyre.

'No. I have to test it with my weight first.'

Alice watches as her father jounces on the tyre, testing to see if it is safe enough for her. She looks up to see the branch shake in sympathy and looks quickly back at her father. What if he were to fall? But he is getting off and lifting her on, her bones as small, white and bendable as birds'.

Alice and John sit in a café in a village in the Lake District. It's early autumn. She holds up a sugar cube between finger and thumb, the light behind it making its crystals the massed cells of an intricate organism under a microscope.

'Did you know,' says John, 'that someone did a chemical analysis of sugar cubes in café sugar bowls and that they found strong traces of blood, semen, faeces and urine?'

She keeps her face serious. 'I didn't know that, no.'

He holds her deadpan gaze until the edges of his mouth are tugged downwards. Alice gets hiccups and he shows her how to cure them by drinking out of the opposite side of a glass. Beyond them, through the window, a plane draws a sheer white line on the sky.

She looks at John's hands, breaking up a bread roll, and suddenly knows she loves him. She looks away, out of the window, and sees for the first time the white line made by the plane. It has by this time drifted into woolliness. She thinks about pointing it out to John, but doesn't.

Alice's sixth summer was hot and dry. Their house had a large garden with the kitchen window looking out over the patio and garden so whenever Alice and her sisters were playing outside they could look up and see their mother watching over them. The freakish heat dried up the reservoirs, previously unheard of in Scotland, and she went with her father to a pump at the end of the street to collect water in round white vats. The water drummed into their empty bottoms. Half-way between the house and the end of the garden was the vegetable patch where peas, potatoes and beetroot pushed their way up from thick, dark soil. On a particularly bright day that summer, Alice stripped off her clothes, scooped up clods of that earth and smeared it in vivid tiger stripes all over her body.

She scared the pious, nervous children next door by roaring at them through the hedge until her mother rapped on the window-pane and shouted at her to stop that at once. She retreated into the undergrowth to collect twigs and leaves to construct a wigwam-shaped lair. Her younger sister stood outside the lair and whinged to be let in. Alice said, only if you are a tiger. Beth looked at the soil and then at her clothes and then at their mother's face in the kitchen window. Alice sat in the moist dark with her stripes, growling and gazing at the triangle of sky visible through the top of the lair.

'You thought you were a little African boy, didn't you?'

She sits in the bath, her hair plastered into dripping spikes, and her grandmother soaps her back and front. The skin of her grandmother's hands feels roughened. The water is grey-brown, full of the garden's soil, lifted off her skin. In the next room she can hear the thrum of her father's voice, talking on the telephone.

'Don't cover yourself in soil again, will you, Alice?'

Her skin looks lighter under the water. Is this what skin looks like when it's dead?

'Alice? Promise me you won't do it again.'

She nods her head, spraying water over the ceramic sides of the yellow bath.

Her grandmother towels her back. 'Wee angel wings,' she says, patting Alice's shoulder-blades dry. 'Everyone was an angel once, and this is where our wings would have been.'

She twists her head around to see the jutting isosceles triangle of bone flex and retract beneath her skin, as if preparing for celestial flight.

Across the café table, John looks at Alice who is looking out of the window. Today she has pulled the weight of her hair away from her face, giving her the appearance of a Spanish *niña* or a flamenco dancer. He imagines her that morning brushing the shining mass of her hair before clipping it at the back of her head. He reaches over the empty coffee mugs and cups the large knot of hair in his palm. She turns her eyes on him in surprise.

'I just wanted to know what it felt like.'

She touches it herself before saying, 'I often think about getting it all cut off.'

'Don't,' John says quickly, 'don't ever cut it off.' The aureoles of her eyes widen in surprise. 'It might contain all your strength,' he jokes feebly. He wants to free it from its silver clasp and bury his face in it. He wants to inhale its smell to the bottom of his lungs. He has caught its scent before. The first time he met her, she was standing in the doorway of his office with a book in her hand, and her hair swung at her waist so cleanly that he fancied it almost made a bell-like note. He wants to edge along its byways and curves in the dark and wake up in its strands.

'Do you want another coffee?' she says, and as she turns to look for the waitress he sees the shorter hairs springing from the nape of her neck.

Sometime after that coffee, John stretched his arms across the table and pressed her head between his hands. 'Alice Raikes,' he said, 'I afraid I'm going to have to kiss you.'

'You're going to have to? she said levelly, although her heart was hammering in her ribcage. 'Do you think now would be a good time to do it, then?'

He made a great show of pretending to think about it, rolling his eyes, creasing his forehead. 'I think now is probably OK.'

Then he kissed her, very gently at first. They kissed for a long time, their fingers entwining. After a while, he pulled back and said, 'I think if we don't go soon, we may be asked to leave. I doubt they'd appreciate us making love on the table.' He was holding on to her hand so tightly that her knucklebones were beginning to hurt. She floundered with her other hand for her bag under the table, but encountered only his legs. He wedged her hand between his knees.

She began to laugh. 'John! Let go!' She struggled to release both her hands but his grip only tightened. He was smiling at her, a puzzled look on his face.

'If you don't let me go we can't leave or make love,' she reasoned.

He released her immediately. 'You are absolutely right.'

He fished her bag off the floor himself and hurried her into her coat. As they walked out of the door, he pressed her to his side, breathing into her hair.

The curtains in the sitting room of their house were of a heavy dark mauve damask, insulated on the outermost side with a thin membrane of yellowing sponge. As a child, Alice took against these curtains. She found it incredibly satisfying to peel away great swatches of the sponge, leaving the mauve material threadbare with light shining through it. One Hallowe'en, after they had scooped out the soft moss of a pumpkin's innards and scored square eyes and a jagged mouth into its skin, Beth and Alice were left reverently gazing at its flicking, demonic glow. Kirsty had eaten too much of the pumpkin scrapings and was being administered to somewhere else in the house. She couldn't say whether she actually planned to burn the curtains but she somehow found herself standing beside them, holding a lit match in a thin-fingered grip, training its curling flame to the curtain's edge. They caught fire with astonishing speed; the damask fizzled away as the flames tore upwards. Beth began to scream, great tongues of flame were licking across the ceiling. Alice jumped up and down in delight and exhilaration, clapping her hands and shouting. Then her mother burst into the room and dragged her away. She shut the door on them and the three of them stood wide-eyed and frozen in the hallway.

Ann runs down the stairs two at a time. Beth's screams are getting louder. They are real screams, full of terror. The sitting room is filled with smoke and the curtains are on fire. Beth hurls herself sobbing at Ann's knees and grips both her legs tightly. Ann is for a moment immobilised and it is then that she sees Alice. She is gazing at the flames, rapt, her whole body contorted and twisted with delight. In her right hand is a spent match. Ann lurches forward and seizes her daughter by the shoulder. Alice struggles in her grasp like a hooked fish. Ann is shocked by her sudden strength. They tussle, Alice spitting and snarling until Ann manages to grip both her hands and drags her kicking to the door. She shuts all three of her children in the hall and then runs to the kitchen for water.

John has fallen into a deep sleep. The rhythm of his breathing is that of a deep-sea diver. His head is resting on Alice's sternum. She sniffs his hair. A slight woody smell like freshly sharpened pencils. Some kind of

shampoo. Lemon? She inhales again. A vague overlay of
the cigarette smoke of the café. She places her hand on
his ribcage and feels the swell and fall of his lungs. The
whispering tick, tick of her own blood sounds against
her eardrums.

She eases herself out from underneath him and hugs
her knees to her chest. She is tempted to wake him up.
She wants to talk. His skin is tanned a light golden
brown all over, except for his groin which is a pale,
vulnerable white. She cups her hand over his penis,
curled against his leg. It twitches in response. She laughs
and covers his body with her own, burying her nose and
mouth in the curve of his neck. 'John? Are you awake?'

The fire was put out by my mother dousing it with water.
The black sooty streaks were to scar the ceiling for years.
Although my parents often talked about redecorating the
room, the fire was never mentioned, never discussed. Not
once did they ask me what had prompted me to set fire
to the curtains.

about the **author**

Maggie O'Farrell

Maggie O'Farrell was born in Northern Ireland but moved with her family to North Berwick when she was 13. After going to university in England she went to London, where she has since lived. Until the publication of her first novel, *After You'd Gone,* she was Deputy Literary Editor for a Sunday newspaper. Her second novel, *My Lover's Lover*, was published in 2002.

Also available:
My Lover's Lover

discussion **points**

1. What effect does O'Farrell achieve by cutting sharply between scenes and stories?

2. Would the mood or impact of the novel be changed by a strictly chronological unfolding of events?

3. Would there be another way of conveying immediacy other than the use of the present tense?

4. In what ways does the author manipulate readers into seeing characters in the light she wants them to?

5. How important is location to the story?

6. Is this novel essentially, or wholly, a tragedy?

press quotes

'Grips the reader from its first dramatic pages...
What begins as a thriller grows and deepens into a
powerful exposé of the ghosts that lie dormant (or just
unmentionable) in the recesses of a family's collective
memory.'
– *Mail on Sunday*

'Filled with the kind of touching, funny details that
make fiction rewarding.'
– *Evening Standard*

'What makes this book remarkable is a luminous use
of language and imagery.'
– *Observer*

'Love in many guises – romantic, familial, unwilling,
redemptive – powers the novel... it's passionate, tender,
and portrayed with a refreshing lack of cynicism... a
compulsively readable and accomplished first novel.'
– *Independent*

'*After You'd Gone* is beautifully written contemporary fiction ... its author has given her subjective story the essential transmutation of art.'
– *Sunday Times*

'Harrowing, profound, and beautifully written.'
– *Independent on Sunday*

'O'Farrell is blessed with a tender, solicitous intelligence ... Honest, moving and wise beyond its author's years.'
– *Time Out*

'Assured and seductive ... in sensitive and almost blood-curdingly honest detail, O'Farrell has constructed a love story dealing with the need to mine the past for clues to the present.'
– *Literary Review*

similar **reads**

Behind the Scenes at the Museum by Kate Atkinson

(Black Swan; ISBN 0552996181)

A complex, anguished but witty saga, stretching back into the family archive, this is the story of a young woman finally making sense of the mystery that has haunted her from her childhood.

Hotel World by Ali Smith

(Penguin Books; ISBN: 0140296794)

The accidental death of a chamber maid in a hotel dumb waiter is the trigger for Smith's whirling dervish of a novel, about grief, desire, and the way the world carries on without missing a beat when a loved one dies, yet for the bereaved, nothing is ever the same again.

The Tin Can Tree by Anne Tyler

(Vintage; ISBN: 0099337002)

The tragic death of young Janie Pike leaves her family devastated by grief and guilt. The effect of her death on each family member is depicted with enormous compassion and strength, showing how finally a way forward becomes possible for each of them.

The Glass Lake by Maeve Binchy
(Orion; ISBN: 1857978013)

In the small and gossipy Irish town of Lough Glass, the beautiful Helen McMahon remains an enigma. When she disappears, presumed drowned in the lake, the lives of her family, especially her daughter Kit, are altered beyond recognition.

Martin Sloane by Michael Redhill
(Vintage; ISBN: 0099438038)

Jolene Iolas falls headlong in love with the man of her dreams, an artist called Martin Sloane. After a short spell of idyllic happiness, Sloane disappears without explanation in the middle of the night. Jolene descends into near annihilating grief, and it is many years before she learns the truth.

Montana 1948 by Larry Watson
(Pan; ISBN: 0330349864)

The events of one summer, when the narrator David Hayden is twelve, prove cataclysmic, turning him almost overnight from boy into adult. As his view of the world, and of his family, is savagely changed, he comes to realise that truth is not what you necessarily believe it to be.

competition

Your chance to win ten contemporary works of fiction signed by their authors.

The *Read Around Books* series was developed by Scottish Book Trust to encourage readers to widen their reading interests and discover writers they had never tried before. Has it been a success? We want to hear from you. Tell us if you have enjoyed this little series or not and if you did, do you have any suggestions for authors who should be included in the series in the future.

Writer to us now with the following information:

Name and address
Email address
Are you a member of a readers' group?
Name of readers' group

Send us the information above and we will enter you into our prize draw to be drawn on 22 August 2003.

Send to:
RAB Draw
Scottish Book Trust
137 Dundee Street
Edinburgh EH11 1BG

scottish **book trust**

What is Scottish Book Trust?

Scottish Book Trust exists to serve readers and writers in Scotland. We work to ensure that everyone has access to good books, and to related resources and opportunities.

We do this in a number of ways:

- By operating the Writers in Scotland Scheme, which funds over 1,400 visits a year by Scottish writers to a variety of institutions and groups
- By supporting Scottish writing through a programme of professional training opportunities for writers
- By publishing a wide variety of resources and leaflets to support readership
- By promoting initiatives such as National Poetry Day and World Book Day
- And through our Book Information Service, providing free advice and support to readers and writers, and the general public.

For more information please visit
www.scottishbooktrust.com

titles **in the series**

Available in the Read Around Books series

Iain Crichton Smith's *Murdo: The Life and Works,*
  by Douglas Gifford

Meaghan Delahunt's *In The Blue House,*
  by Gavin Wallace

Michel Faber's *Under the Skin,* by Mary Firth

Jonathan Falla's *Blue Poppies,* by Rosemary Goring

Janice Galloway's *Clara,* by David Robinson

Andrew Greig's *That Summer,* by Alan Taylor

Anne MacLeod's *The Dark Ship,* by Lindsey Fraser

Maggie O'Farrell's *After You'd Gone,* by Rosemary Goring

Suhayl Saadi's *The Burning Mirror,*
  by Catherine McInerney

Ali Smith's *Hotel World,* by Kathryn Ross

Muriel Spark's *The Comforters,* by Alan Taylor

Alexander Trocchi's *Young Adam,* by Gillian Mackay